Q & A's About:

The Holy Spirit

By: Only A. Guy

Hard Questions About: The Holy Spirit

Published by VIP Ink Publishing

Cover Art and Editing By Whyte Lady Designs L.L.C.

www.onlyaguy.com
www.facebook.com/onlyaguy
www.twitter.com/onlyaguy1

www.vipinkpublishing.com

ISBN 13: 978-0-9847382-3-6
ISBN: 0-9847382-3-6

Printed in the USA.

If you like this book here are some others coming out by this author you may find enjoyable as well as educational:

2011
HARD QUESTIONS ABOUT GOD
HARD QUESTIONS ABOUT JESUS
THE BOOK OF PRAYERS

2012
HARD QUESTIONS ABOUT THE HOLY SPIRIT
HARD QUESTIONS ABOUT HEAVEN AND HELL
HARD QUESTIONS ABOUT ANGELS AND DEMONS
HARD QUESTIONS ABOUT SALVATION
HOPE IN A LOST AND FALLEN WORLD

2013
HARD QUESTIONS ABOUT THE END TIMES
HARD QUESTIONS ABOUT CHRISTIANITY
HARD QUESTIONS ABOUT CREATION
HARD QUESTIONS ABOUT HUMANITY

2014
HARD QUESTIONS ABOUT LIFE'S DECISIONS
HARD QUESTIONS ABOUT CULTS AND RELIGIONS
HARD QUESTIONS ABOUT FALSE DOCTRINE
HARD QUESTIONS ABOUT PRAYER
HARD QUESTIONS ABOUT SIN

1. Question: "Who is the Holy Spirit?"

There are many misconceptions on the identity of the Holy Spirit. Some view the Holy Spirit as a mystical force. Others understand the Holy Spirit as the impersonal power God makes available to followers of Christ. What does the Bible say about the identity of the Holy Spirit? Simply put - the Bible says that the Holy Spirit is God. The Bible also tells us that the Holy Spirit is a Person, a Being with a mind, emotions, and a will.

The fact that the Holy Spirit is God is clearly seen in many Scriptures including *Acts 5:3-4*. In this verse Peter confronts Ananias as to why he had lied to the Holy Spirit and tells him that he had *"not lied to men but to God."* It is a clear declaration that lying to the Holy Spirit is lying to God. We can also know that the Holy Spirit is God because He possesses the attributes or characteristics of God. For example, the fact that the Holy Spirit is omnipresent is seen in *Psalm 139:7-8, "Where can I go from Your Spirit? Or where can I flee from Your presence? If I ascend into heaven, You are there; If I make my bed in hell, behold, You are there."* Then in *1 Corinthians 2:10*, we see the characteristic of omniscience in the Holy Spirit. *"But God has revealed them to us through His Spirit. For the Spirit searches all things, yes, the deep things of God. For what man knows the things of a man except the spirit of the man which is in him? Even so no one knows the things of God except the Spirit of God."*

We can know that the Holy Spirit is indeed a Person because He possesses a mind, emotions, and a will. The Holy Spirit thinks and knows *(1 Corinthians 2:10)*. The Holy Spirit can be grieved *(Ephesians 4:30)*. The Spirit intercedes for us *(Romans 8:26-27)*. The Holy Spirit makes decisions according to His will *(1 Corinthians 12:7-11)*. The Holy Spirit is God, the third "Person" of the Trinity. As God, the Holy Spirit can truly function as the Comforter and Counselor that Jesus promised He would be *(John 14:16,26; 15:26)*.

2. Question: "What is the blasphemy against the Holy Spirit?"

The case of "blasphemy against the Spirit" in the New Testament is mentioned in *Mark 3:22-30* and in *Matthew 12:22-32*. The term blasphemy may be generally defined as "defiant irreverence." We would apply the term to such sins as cursing God, or willfully degrading things relating to God. It is also attributing some evil to God, or denying Him some good that we should attribute to Him. This case of blasphemy, however, is a specific one, called *"THE blasphemy against the Holy Spirit"* in *Matthew 12:31*. In *Matthew 12:31-32*, the Pharisees, having witnessed irrefutable proof that Jesus was working miracles in the power of the Holy Spirit, claimed instead that the Lord was possessed by the demon "Beelzebub" *(Matthew 12:24)*. Now notice that in *Mark 3:30* Jesus is very specific about what exactly they did to commit *"the blasphemy against the Holy Spirit."*

This blasphemy has to do with someone accusing Jesus Christ of being demon-possessed instead of Spirit-filled. There are other ways to blaspheme the Holy Spirit, but this was "THE" unpardonable blasphemy. As a result, the blasphemy against the Holy Spirit cannot be duplicated today. Jesus Christ is not on earth. but seated at the right Hand of God. No one can witness Jesus Christ performing a miracle and then attribute that power to Satan instead of the Spirit. Although there is no blasphemy of the Spirit today, we should always keep in mind there is an unpardonable state of existence, the state of continued unbelief. There is no pardon for a person who dies in unbelief. Continual rejection of the Holy Spirit's promptings to trust in Jesus Christ is the unpardonable blasphemy. Remember what is stated in *John 3:16, "For God so loved the world that he gave his only begotten Son, that whosoever believeth in him should not perish but have eternal life."* The only condition when someone would have no forgiveness is if that someone is not among the *"whoever believes in Him."*

3. Question: "What is Pneumatology?"

The word Pneumatology comes from two Greek words which mean "wind, air, spirit" and "word" - combining to mean "the study of the

Holy Spirit." Pneumatology is the study of God the Holy Spirit, the third Person of the Trinity. It answers numerous important questions about the Holy Spirit:

- Who/what is the Holy Spirit? There are many misconceptions about the identity of the Holy Spirit. Some view the Holy Spirit as a mystical force. Others understand the Holy Spirit as the impersonal power God makes available to followers of Christ. What does the Bible say about the identity of the Holy Spirit?
- When/How do we receive the Holy Spirit? This discussion is controversial because the ministries of the Holy Spirit are often confused. The receiving / indwelling of the Spirit occurs at the moment of salvation. The filling of the Spirit is an ongoing process in the Christian life.
- What is the baptism of the Holy Spirit? The baptism of the Holy Spirit may be defined as that work whereby the Spirit of God places the believer into union with Christ and into union with other believers in the Body of Christ at the moment of salvation.
- How can I be filled with the Spirit? It is important to distinguish between the indwelling and filling of the Spirit. The permanent indwelling of the Spirit is not for a select few believers, but rather for all believers. This is in contrast to the commanded filling of the Spirit found in *Ephesians 5:18*.
- Are the miraculous gifts of the Spirit for today? This is not a question of can the Holy Spirit give someone a miraculous gift. The question is does the Holy Spirit still dispense the miraculous gifts today. Above all else, we entirely recognize that the Holy Spirit is free to dispense gifts according to His will *(1 Corinthians 12:7-11)*.
- Many Christians have an unbiblical perception of the Holy Spirit. Some understand the Holy Spirit as a power or force given to us from God. This is not Biblical. Pneumatology teaches us that the Holy Spirit is a Person, with a mind, emotions, and will. The Holy Spirit is Jesus' "replacement" on earth *(John 14:16-26; 15:26; 16:7)*. The Holy Spirit is received at salvation *(Romans 8:9)* and is the permanent possession of every believer in Christ *(Ephesians 1:13-14)*. Pneumatology helps us to understand these issues and recognize the Biblical roles of the Holy Spirit in our lives today.

- The study of Pneumatology is of immense benefit to the Christian. In the pages of Scripture, we come face to face with the third Person of the trinity, God himself in spirit, and we see His very personal and intimate ministry to us. Through Him, we come to know God's love for us *"because the love of God has been poured out in our hearts by the Holy Spirit who was given to us" (Romans 5:5)*. To understand the ministry of the Holy Spirit is to find joy in His role as our Comforter *(John 16:7; Acts 9:31)* who not only helps and comforts us, but who comes to our rescue when our hearts are so burdened we cannot even pray for relief *(Romans 8:26)*. When we pursue the knowledge of the Holy Spirit we find, to our great delight, that He not only lives within us, but He does so forever, never to leave or forsake us *(John 14:16)*. All these truths are burned into our hearts when we study Pneumatology.
- A good summary verse for Pneumatology is *John 16:8-11, "When He (the Holy Spirit) comes, He will convict the world of guilt in regard to sin and righteousness and judgment: in regard to sin, because men do not believe in me; in regard to righteousness, because I am going to the Father, where you can see me no longer; and in regard to judgment, because the prince of this world now stands condemned."*

4. Question: "When/How do we receive the Holy Spirit?"

The Apostle Paul clearly taught that we receive the Holy Spirit the moment we believe in Jesus Christ as our Savior. *1 Corinthians 12:13* declares, *"For we were all baptized by one Spirit into one body-whether Jews or Greeks, slave or free - and we were all given the one Spirit to drink." Romans 8:9* tells us that if a person does not possess the Holy Spirit, he or she does not belong to Christ; *"You, however, are controlled not by the sinful nature but by the Spirit, if the Spirit of God lives in you. And if anyone does not have the Spirit of Christ, he does not belong to Christ." Ephesians 1:13-14* teaches us that the Holy Spirit is the seal of salvation for all those who believe, *"Having believed, you were marked in him with a seal, the promised Holy Spirit, who is a deposit guaranteeing our inheritance until the redemption of those who are God's possession-to the praise of his glory."*

These three Scriptures make it clear that the Holy Spirit must be received at the moment of salvation. Paul could not say that we all were baptized by one Spirit and all given one Spirit to drink if not all of the Corinthian believers possessed the Holy Spirit. *Romans 8:9* is even stronger. If a person does not have the Spirit, he does not belong to Christ. Therefore, the possession of the Spirit is an identifying factor of the possession of salvation. Further, the Holy Spirit could not be the *"seal of salvation" (Ephesians 1:13-14)* if He is not received at the moment of salvation. Many Scriptures make it abundantly clear that our salvation is secured the moment we receive Christ as Savior.

This discussion is controversial because the ministries of the Holy Spirit are often confused. The receiving/indwelling of the Spirit occurs at the moment of salvation. The filling of the Spirit is an ongoing process in the Christian life. While we hold that the baptism of the Spirit also occurs at the moment of salvation, some Christians do not. This sometimes results in the baptism of the Spirit being confused with "receiving the Spirit" as an act subsequent to salvation. In conclusion, how do we receive the Holy Spirit? We receive the Holy Spirit by simply believing in the Lord Jesus Christ as our Savior *(John 3:5-16)*. When do we receive the Holy Spirit? The Holy Spirit becomes our permanent possession the moment we believe.

5. Question: "Are the miraculous gifts of the Spirit for today?"

First, it is important to recognize that this is not a question of whether God still performs miracles today. It would be foolish and unbiblical to claim that God does not heal people, speak to people, and perform miraculous signs and wonders today. The question is whether the miraculous gifts of the Spirit, described primarily in *1 Corinthians chapters 12-14*, are still active in the church today. This is also not a question of "can" the Holy Spirit give someone a miraculous gift. The question is "does" the Holy Spirit still dispense the miraculous gifts today. Above all else, we entirely recognize that the Holy Spirit is free to dispense gifts according to His will *(1 Corinthians 12:7-11)*.

In the book of Acts and the Epistles, the vast majority of miracles are performed by the apostles and their close associates. *2 Corinthians 12:12* gives us the reason why, *"The things that mark an apostle, signs, wonders and miracles, were done among you with great perseverance."* If every believer in Christ was equipped with the ability to perform signs, wonders, and miracles - signs, wonders, and miracles could in no way be the identifying marks of an apostle. *Acts 2:22* tells us that Jesus was "accredited" by "miracles, wonders, and signs." Similarly were the apostles "marked" as genuine messengers from God by the miracles they performed. *Acts 14:3* describes the Gospel message being "confirmed" by the miracles Paul and Barnabas performed.

1 Corinthians chapters 12-14 deal primarily with the subject of the gifts of the Spirit. It seems from that text that "ordinary" Christians were sometimes given miraculous gifts *(12:8-10; 28-30)*. We are not told how commonplace this was. From what we learned above, that the apostles were "marked" by signs and wonders, it would seem that miraculous gifts being given to "ordinary" Christians was the exception, not the rule. Outside of the apostles and their close associates, the New Testament nowhere specifically describes individuals exercising the miraculous gifts of the Spirit.

It is also important to realize that the early church did not have the completed Bible, as we do today *(2 Timothy 3:16-17)*. Therefore, the gifts of prophecy, knowledge, wisdom, etc. were necessary in order for the early Christians to know what God would have them to do. The gift of prophecy enabled believers to communicate new truth and revelation from God. Now that God's revelation is complete in the Bible, the "revelatory" gifts are no longer needed, at least not in the same capacity as they were in the New Testament.

God miraculously heals people every day. God still speaks to us today, whether in an audible voice, whether in our minds, or whether through impressions and feelings. God still does amazing miracles, signs, and wonders - and sometimes performs those miracles through a Christian. However, what was just described are not necessarily the miraculous gifts of the Spirit. The primary purpose of the miraculous gifts was to prove that the Gospel was true and that the apostles were truly God's messengers. The Bible does not say outright that the miraculous gifts have ceased, but it does lay the foundation for why they might no longer be necessary.

6. Question: "What is the gift of speaking in tongues?"

The first occurrence of speaking in tongues occurred on the Day of Pentecost in *Acts 2:1-4*. The apostles went out and shared the Gospel with the crowds, speaking to them in their own languages, *"we hear them declaring the wonders of God in our own tongues!" (Acts 2:11)*. The Greek word translated "tongues" literally means "languages." Therefore, the gift of tongues is speaking in a language a person does not know in order to minister to someone who does speak that language. In *1 Corinthians chapters 12-14*, where Paul discusses miraculous gifts, he comments that, *"Now, brothers, if I come to you and speak in tongues, what good will I be to you, unless I bring you some revelation or knowledge or prophecy or word of instruction?" (1 Corinthians 14:6)*. According to the Apostle Paul, and in agreement with the tongues described in *Acts*, speaking in tongues is valuable to the one hearing God's message in his/her own language, but it is useless to everyone else unless it is interpreted/translated.

A person with the gift of interpreting tongues *(1 Corinthians 12:30)* could understand what a tongues-speaker was saying even though he/she did not know the language that was being spoken. The tongues-interpreter would then communicate the message of the tongues-speaker to everyone else, so all could understand. *"For this reason anyone who speaks in a tongue should pray that he may interpret what he says" (1 Corinthians 14:13)*. Paul's conclusion regarding un-interpreted tongues is powerful, *"But in the church I would rather speak five intelligible words to instruct others than ten thousand words in a tongue" (1 Corinthians 14:19)*.

Is the gift of tongues for today? *1 Corinthians 13:8* mentions the gift of tongues ceasing, although it connects the ceasing with the arrival of the "perfect" in *1 Corinthians 13:10*. Some point to a difference in the language in prophecy and knowledge "ceasing" with tongues "being ceased" as evidence for tongues ceasing before the arrival of the "perfect." While possible, this is not explicitly clear from the text. Some also point to passages such as *Isaiah 28:11* and *Joel 2:28-29* as evidence that speaking in tongues was a sign of God's oncoming judgment. *1 Corinthians 14:22* describes tongues as a "sign to unbelievers." According to this argument, the gift of tongues was a warning to the Jews that God was going to judge Israel for rejecting Jesus Christ as Messiah. Therefore, when God did in fact judge Israel (with the destruction of Jerusalem by the Romans in A.D. 70), the gift of tongues would no longer serve its intended purpose. While this view is possible, the primary purpose of tongues being fulfilled does not necessarily demand its cessation. Scripture does not conclusively assert that the gift of speaking in tongues has ceased.

At the same time, if the gift of speaking in tongues were active in the church today, it would be performed in agreement with Scripture. It would be a real and intelligible language *(1 Corinthians 14:10)*. It would be for the purpose of communicating God's Word with a person of another language *(Acts 2:6-12)*. It would be in agreement with the command that God gave through the Apostle Paul, *"If anyone speaks in a tongue, two, or at the most three, should speak, one at a time, and someone must interpret. If there is no interpreter, the speaker should keep quiet in the church and speak to himself and God" (1 Corinthians 14:27-28)*. It would also be in submission to *1 Corinthians 14:33, "For God is not the author of confusion, but of peace, as in all churches of the saints."*

God most definitely can give a person the gift of speaking in tongues to enable him/her to communicate with a person who speaks another language. The Holy Spirit is sovereign in the dispersion of the spiritual gifts *(1 Corinthians 12:11)*. Just imagine how much more productive missionaries could be if they didn't have to go to language school, and were instantly able to speak to people in their own language. However, God does not seem to be doing this. Tongues does not seem to occur today in the form it did in the New Testament despite the fact that it would be immensely useful. The vast majority of believers who claim to practice the gift of speaking in tongues do not do so in agreement with the Scriptures mentioned above. These facts lead to the conclusion that the gift of tongues has ceased, or is at least a rarity in God's plan for the church today.

7. Question: "How do I know what my spiritual gift is?"

There is no magic formula or spiritual gift test that can tell us exactly what our spiritual gifts are. The Holy Spirit distributes the gifts as He determines *(1 Corinthians 12:7-11)*. At the same time, God does not want us to be ignorant of how He wants us to serve Him. The problem is that it is very easy for us to get so caught up in spiritual gifts that we only seek to serve God in the area in which we feel we have a spiritual gift. That is not how the spiritual gifts work. God calls us to obediently serve Him. He will equip us with whatever gift or gifts we need to accomplish the task or tasks He has called us to.

Identifying our spiritual giftedness can be accomplished in various ways. Spiritual gift tests or inventories, while not to be fully relied upon, can definitely help us understand where our gifting might be. Confirmation from others also gives light to our spiritual giftedness. Other people who see us serving the Lord can often identify a spiritual gift in use that we might take for granted or not recognize. Prayer is also important. The one person who knows exactly how we are spiritually gifted is the gift-giver Himself – the Holy Spirit. We can ask God to show us how we are gifted, that we might better use our spiritual gifts for His glory.

Yes, God calls some to be teachers and gives them the gift of teaching. God calls some to be servants and blesses them with the gift of helps. However, specifically knowing our spiritual gift does not excuse us from serving God in areas outside our gifting. Is it beneficial to know what spiritual gift(s) God has given us? Of course it is. Is it wrong to focus so much on spiritual gifts that we miss other opportunities to serve God? Yes! If we are dedicated to being used by God, He will equip us with the spiritual gifts we need.

8. Question: "How does God distribute spiritual gifts?"

Romans 12:3-8 and *1 Corinthians 12* make it clear that each Christian is given spiritual gifts according to the Lord's choice. Spiritual gifts are given for the purpose of the edification of the body of Christ *(1 Corinthians 12:7; 14:12)*. The exact timing of when these gifts are given is not specifically mentioned. Most assume that spiritual gifts are given at the time of spiritual birth (the moment of salvation). However, there are some verses that may indicate that God sometimes gives spiritual gifts later as well. Both *1 Timothy 4:14* and *2 Timothy 1:6* refer to a *"gift"* that Timothy had received at the time of his ordination *"by prophecy.*" This likely indicates that one of the elders at Timothy's ordination spoke under God's influence of a spiritual gift that Timothy would have as an enablement for his future ministry.

We are also told in *1 Corinthians 12:28-31* and in *1 Corinthians 14:12 -13* that it is God, not us, who chooses the gifts. These passages also indicate that not everyone will have a particular gift. Paul tells the Corinthian believers that if they are going to covet or long after spiritual gifts, they should set aside their fascination with the "spectacular" or "showy" gifts, and instead strive after the more edifying gifts, such as prophesying, speaking forth the word of God for the building up of others. Now, why would Paul tell them to strongly desire the "best" gifts if they already had been given all that they would be given, and there was no further opportunity of gaining these "best" gifts? It may lead one to believe that even as Solomon sought wisdom from God in order to be a good ruler over God's people, so God will grant to us those gifts that we need in order to be of greater benefit to His church.

Having said this, it still remains that these gifts are distributed according to God's choosing, not our own. If every Corinthian strongly desired a particular gift, such as prophesying, God would not give everyone that gift simply because they strongly desired it. Why? Where would be those who are needed to serve all of the other functions of the body of Christ?

There is one thing that is abundantly clear, God's command is God's enablement. If God commands us to do something, such as witness, love the unlovely, disciple the nations, etc., He will enable us to do it. Some may not be as "gifted" at evangelism as others, but God commands all Christians to witness and disciple *(Matthew 28:18-20; Acts 1:8).* We are all called to evangelize whether or not we have the spiritual gift of evangelism. A determined Christian who strives after learning the Word and developing his teaching ability will become a better teacher than one who may have the spiritual gift of teaching, but who neglects the gift.

In summary, are spiritual gifts given to us when we receive Christ, or are they cultivated through our walk with God? The answer is both. Normally, spiritual gifts are given at salvation, but also need to be cultivated through spiritual growth. Can a desire in your heart be pursued and developed into your spiritual gift? Can you seek after certain spiritual gifts? *1 Corinthians 12:31* seems to indicate that this is possible, *"earnestly desire the best gifts."* You can seek from God a spiritual gift and be zealous after it by seeking to develop that area. At the same time, if it is not God's will, you will not receive a certain spiritual gift no matter how strongly you seek after it. God is infinitely wise, and knows with which gifts you will be most productive for His kingdom.

No matter how much we have been gifted with one gift or another, we are all called upon to develop a number of areas mentioned in the lists of spiritual gifts; to be hospitable, to show acts of mercy, to serve one another, to evangelize, etc. As we seek to serve Him out of love, for the purpose of building up others for His glory, He will bring glory to His name, grow His church, and reward us *(1 Corinthians 3:5-8; 12:31 -14:1)*. God promises that as we make Him our delight, He will give us the desires of our heart *(Psalm 37:4-5)*. This would surely include preparing us to serve Him in a way that will bring us purpose and satisfaction.

9. Question: "Is being slain in the Spirit biblical?"

The idea of being "slain in the Spirit" is when a minister lays hands on someone, and that person collapses to the floor, supposedly being overcome in the power of the Spirit. Those who practice "slaying in the Spirit" use Bible passages that talk about people becoming *"as dead" (Revelation 1:17)* or of falling upon their faces *(Ezekiel 1:28; Daniel 8:17-18; Daniel 10:7-9)*. However, there are a number of contrasts between this biblical "falling on one's face" and the practice of "being slain in the Spirit."

1. The biblical falling down was a result of a person's reaction to what he saw in a vision or that was beyond ordinary happenings, such as at the transfiguration of Christ *(Matthew 17:6)*. In the unbiblical practice of "being slain," the person responds to another's "touch" or to the motion of the speaker's arm.
2. The biblical instances were few and far between, such that they occurred only rarely in the lives of but a few. In the "being slain" phenomenon, falling down is a weekly event in their churches and an experience that happens to many.
3. In the biblical instances, the people fall upon their faces in

awe at either what they see or Whom they see. In the "slain in the Spirit" counterfeit, they fall backwards, either in response to the wave of the speaker's arm or as a result of a church leader's touch (or push in some cases).

4. We are not claiming that all examples of being "slain in the Spirit" are fakes or responses to a touch or push. Many people experience an energy or a force that causes them to fall back. However, we find no Biblical basis for this concept. Yes, there may be some energy or force involved, but if so, it is very likely not of God, and not the result of the working of the Holy Spirit.

It is unfortunate that people look to such bizarre counterfeits that produce no spiritual fruit, rather than pursuing the practical fruit which the Spirit gives us for the purpose of glorifying Christ with our lives *(Galatians 5:22-23)*. Being filled with the Spirit is not evidenced by such counterfeits, but by a life that overflows with the Word of God such that the Word spills over in spiritual songs and thanksgiving to God. May *Ephesians 5:18-20* and *Galatians 5:22-23* so picture our lives!

10. Question: "What is the baptism of the Holy Spirit?"

The baptism of the Holy Spirit may be defined as that work whereby the Spirit of God places the believer into union with Christ and into union with other believers in the Body of Christ at the moment of salvation. *1 Corinthians 12:12-13* and *Romans 6:1-4* are the central passages in the Bible where we find this doctrine. *1 Corinthians 12:13* states, *"For by one Spirit we were all baptized into one body, whether Jews or Greeks, whether slaves or free, and we were all made to drink of one Spirit." Romans 6:1-4* states, *"What shall we say then? Are we to continue in sin so that grace may increase? May it never be! How shall we who died to sin still live in it? Or do you not know that all of us who have been baptized into Christ Jesus have been baptized into His death? Therefore we have been buried with Him through baptism into death, so that as Christ was raised from the dead through the glory of the Father, so we too might walk in newness of life."* Even though *Romans 6* does not mention specifically the Spirit of God, it does describe believers positionally before God and *1 Corinthians 12* tells us how that happens.

Three facts are necessary to look into that help solidify our understanding of Spirit baptism:

- First, *1 Corinthians 12:13* clearly states that all have been baptized just as all have made to drink (the indwelling of the Spirit).
- Second, nowhere in Scripture does it exhort believers to be baptized with/in/by the Spirit. This indicates that all believers have experienced this ministry.
- Last, *Ephesians 4:5* seems to refer to Spirit baptism. If this is the case, Spirit baptism is the reality of every believer, just as "one faith" and "one Father" are.

In conclusion, the baptism of the Holy Spirit does two things,

1. it joins us to the Body of Christ, and
2. it actualizes our co-crucifixion with Christ.

Being in His body means we are risen with Him to newness of life *(Romans 6:4)*. We should then exercise our spiritual gifts to keep that body functioning properly as stated in the context of *1 Corinthians 12:13*. Experiencing the one Spirit baptism serves as the basis for keeping the unity of the church, as in the context of *Ephesians 4:5*. Being associated with Christ in His death, burial, and resurrection through Spirit baptism establishes the basis for realizing our separation from the power of indwelling sin and our walk in newness of life *(Romans 6:1-10, Colossians 2:12)*.

11. Question: "What is the role of the Holy Spirit in our lives today?"

After the gift of salvation through Jesus Christ, of all the other gifts given to mankind by God, there is none greater than the presence of the Holy Spirit. The Spirit has many functions, roles, and activities. First,

He does a work in the hearts of all people everywhere. Jesus told the disciples that He would send the Spirit into the world to *"convict the world concerning sin, and concerning righteousness, and concerning judgment" (John 16:7-11)*. Everyone has a "God consciousness," whether they admit it or not, because the Spirit applies the truths of God to men's own minds as to convince them by fair and sufficient arguments that they are sinners. Responding to that conviction brings men to salvation.

Once we are saved and belong to God, the Spirit takes up residence in our hearts forever, sealing us with the confirming, certifying, and assuring pledge of our eternal state as His children. Jesus said He would send the Spirit to us to be our Helper, Comforter, and Guide. *"And I will pray the Father and He will give you another Helper that He may abide with you forever" (John 14:16)*. The Greek word translated here "Helper" means one who is called alongside and has the idea of someone who encourages and exhorts. "Abiding" has to do with His permanent residence in the hearts of believers *(Romans 8:9; 1 Corinthians 6:19, 20; 12:13)*. Jesus gave the Spirit as a "compensation" for His absence, to perform the functions toward us which He would have done if He had remained personally with us.

Among those functions is that of revealer of truth. The Spirit's presence within us enables us to understand and interpret the Word. Jesus told His disciples *"when He, the Spirit of Truth, has come, He will guide you into all truth" (John 16:13)*. He reveals to our minds the whole counsel of God as it relates to worship, doctrine, and Christian living. He is the ultimate guide, going before, leading the way, removing obstructions, opening the understanding, and making all things plain and clear. He leads in the way we should go in all spiritual things. Without such a guide, we would be apt to fall into error. A crucial part of the Truth He reveals is that Jesus is who He said He is *(John 15:26; 1 Corinthians 12:3)*. The Spirit convinces us of Christ's deity and sonship, His incarnation, His being the Messiah, His sufferings and death, His resurrection and ascension, His exaltation at the right hand of God, and His role as the Judge of all. He gives glory to Christ in all things *(John 16:14)*.

Another of His roles is that of gift-giver. First Corinthians 12 describes the spiritual gifts given to believers in order that we may function as the body of Christ on earth. All these gifts, both great and small, are given by the Spirit so that we may be His ambassadors to the world, showing forth His grace and glorifying Him.

The Spirit also functions as fruit-producer in our lives. When He indwells us, He begins the work of harvesting His fruit in our lives - love, joy, peace, long-suffering, kindness, goodness, faith, meekness, and self-control *(Galatians 5:22-23)*. These are not works of our flesh, which is incapable of producing such fruit, but they are products of the Spirit's presence in our lives.

The knowledge that the Holy Spirit of God has taken up residence in our lives, that He performs all these miraculous functions, that He dwells with us forever and will never leave or forsake us is cause for great joy and comfort. Thank God for this precious Gift – the Holy Spirit and His work in our lives!

12. Question: "How can I be filled with the Holy Spirit?"

A key verse that discusses the filling of the Holy Spirit in this age is *John 14:16*, where Jesus promised the Spirit would indwell believers and that the indwelling would be permanent. It is important to distinguish the indwelling and filling of the Spirit. The permanent indwelling of the Spirit is not for a select few believers, but rather for all believers. There are a number of references in Scripture that supports this conclusion. The first is that the Holy Spirit is a gift given to all believers in Jesus without exception, and no conditions are placed upon this gift except faith in Christ *(John 7:37-39)*. The second is that the Holy Spirit is given at salvation. *Ephesians 1:13* indicates that the Holy Spirit is given at the moment of salvation. *Galatians 3:2* also emphasizes this same truth, saying that the sealing and indwelling with the Spirit took place at the time of believing. Third, the Holy Spirit indwells believers permanently. The Holy Spirit is given to believers as a down payment, or verification of their future glorification in Christ *(2 Corinthians 1:22; Ephesians 4:30)*.

This is in contrast to the filling of the Spirit command found in *Ephesians 5:18*. We should be so completely yielded to the Holy Spirit that He can possess us fully, and in that sense, fill us. *Romans 8:9* and

Ephesians 1:13-14 state that He dwells within every believer, but He can be grieved *(Ephesians 4:30)*, and His activity within us can be quenched *(1 Thessalonians 5:19)*. When we allow this to happen, we do not experience the fullness of the Holy Spirit's working and power in and through us. To be filled with the Spirit implies freedom for Him to occupy every part of our lives, guiding and controlling us. His power then can be exerted through us so that what we do is fruitful to God. The filling of the Spirit does not apply to outward acts alone; it also applies to the innermost thoughts and motives of our actions. *Psalm 19:14* says, *"Let the words of my mouth, and the meditation of my heart, be acceptable to you, O Lord my strength, and my redeemer."*

Sin is what separates us from the filling of the Holy Spirit, and obedience to God is how the filling of the Spirit is maintained. Although our focus should be to be filled as *Ephesians 5:18* commands, praying for the filling of the Holy Spirit is not what accomplishes the filling of the Spirit. Only our obedience to God's commands allows the Spirit freedom to work within us. Because we are sinful creatures, it is impossible to be filled with the Spirit all of the time. We should immediately deal with sin in our lives, and renew our commitment to being Spirit-filled and Spirit-led.

13. Question: "What is the difference between a talent and a spiritual gift?"

There are similarities and differences between talents and spiritual gifts. Both are gifts from God. Both grow in effectiveness with use. Both are intended to be used on behalf of others, not for selfish purposes. *1 Corinthians 12:7* states that spiritual gifts are given to benefit others, not one's self. As the two great commandments deal with loving God and others, it follows that one should use his talents for that purpose. But talents and spiritual gifts differ in whom they are given to and when. Regardless of his belief in God or in Christ, a person is given a natural talent as a result of a combination of genetics (some have natural ability in music, art, or mathematics) and surroundings (growing up in a musical family will aid one in developing a talent for music), or because God desired to endow certain individuals with certain talents (for example, Bazeleel in *Exodus 31:1-6*). Spiritual gifts are given to believers by the Holy Spirit *(Romans 12:3, 6)* at the time of their placing their faith in Christ for the forgiveness of their sins. At that time the Holy Spirit gives to the new believer the spiritual gift(s) He desires the believer to have *(1 Corinthians 12:11)*. There are three main lists of spiritual gifts:

- *Romans 12:3-8* lists the spiritual gifts as follows: prophecy, serving others (in a general sense), teaching, exhorting, generosity, leadership, and showing mercy.
- *1 Corinthians 12:8-11* lists the gifts as: the word of wisdom (ability to communicate spiritual wisdom), the word of knowledge (ability to communicate practical truth), faith (unusual reliance upon God), the working of miracles, prophecy, discerning of spirits, tongues (ability to speak in a language that one has not studied), and interpretation of tongues.
- The third list is found in *Ephesians 4:10-12*, which speaks of God giving to His church apostles, prophets, evangelists, and pastor-teachers. There is also a question as to how many spiritual gifts there are, as no two lists are the same. It is also possible that the Biblical lists are not exhaustive, that there are additional spiritual gifts beyond the ones the Bible mentions.

While often one may develop his talents and later direct his profession or hobby along those lines, spiritual gifts were given by the Holy Spirit for the building up of Christ's church. In that, all Christians are to play an active part in the furtherance of the gospel of Christ. All are called and equipped to be involved in the *"work of the ministry" (Ephesians 4:12)*. All are gifted so that they can contribute to the cause of Christ out of gratitude for all He has done for them. In doing so, they also find fulfillment in life through their labor for Christ. It is the job of the church leaders to help build up the saints so they can be further equipped for the ministry that God has called them to. The intended result of spiritual gifts is that the church as a whole can grow, being strengthened by the combined supply of each and every member of Christ's body.

To summarize the differences between spiritual gifts and talents:

1. A talent is the result of genetics and/or training, while a spiritual gift is the result of the power of the Holy Spirit.

2. A talent can be possessed by anyone, Christian or non-Christian, while spiritual gifts are only possessed by Christians.

While both talents and spiritual gifts should be used for God's glory and to minister to others, spiritual gifts are focused on these tasks, while talents can be used entirely for non-spiritual purposes.

14. Question: "What is the meaning of "perfect" in 1 Corinthians 13:10?"

1 Corinthians 13:10 says: *"But when that which is perfect has come, then that which is in part will be done away." "That which is in part"* refers to the gifts of prophecy, knowledge and tongues *(vs. 8-9)*. What Paul is saying is that there will be a time when these sign gifts will cease because something better (the "perfect") will replace them. There is some debate as to what the word "perfect" refers to. The two most common views are the completion of the Bible and the glorification of believers in heaven.

There is a difference between how prophecy and knowledge come to an end, and how the gift of languages (tongues) does, as indicated by the Greek verb forms used. Note: Prophecy does not mean forecasting or telling the future. The gift of prophecy in its true biblical definition means simply "speaking forth," or "proclaiming publicly" to which the connotation of prediction was added sometime in the Middle Ages. Since the completion of Scripture, prophecy has not been a means of new revelation, but is limited to proclaiming what has already been revealed in the written Word.

Prophecy and knowledge are both said to "be abolished," the verb indicating that something will put an end to those two functions. What will abolish knowledge and prophecy, according to *verses 9 and 10*, is "that which is perfect." When that occurs, those gifts will be rendered inoperative. The "perfect" is not the completion of Scripture, since there is still the operation of those two gifts and will be in the future kingdom *(Joel 2:28; Acts 2:17; Revelation 11:3)*. The Scriptures do not allow us to see "face to face" or have perfect knowledge as God does *(v. 12)*.

The "perfect" is not the rapture of the church or the second coming of Christ, since the kingdom to follow these events will have an abundance of preachers and teachers *(Isaiah 29:18; 32:3, 4; Joel 2:28; Revelation 11:3)*. The perfect, therefore, must be the eternal state, when we in glory see God face to face *(Revelation 22:4)* and have full knowledge in the eternal new heavens and new earth. Just as a child grows to full understanding, believers will come to perfect knowledge and no such gifts will be necessary.

On the other hand, Paul uses a different word for the end of the gift of languages, thus indicating it will "cease" by itself, rather than being abolished by something, as it did at the end of the apostolic age. It will not end by the coming of the "perfect," for it will already have ceased. The uniqueness of the gift of languages and its interpretations was, as all sign gifts, to authenticate the message and messages of the gospel before the NT was completed *(Hebrews 2:3, 4)*. "Tongues" was also limited by being a judicial sign from God of Israel's judgment *(Isaiah 28:11, 12)*. Tongues was also not a sign to believers, but unbelievers, specifically the unbelieving Jews. Tongues also ceased because there was no need to verify the true messages from God once the Scripture was given. The Bible, not the sign gifts, became the standard by which messages all are to be verified. Tongues was a means of edification in a way far inferior to preaching and teaching. In fact, *chap. 14* was designed to show the Corinthians, so preoccupied with tongues, that it was an inferior means of communication *(vv. 1–12)*, an inferior means of praise *(vv. 13–19)*, and an inferior means of evangelism *(vv. 20–25)*. Prophecy was and is, far superior *(vv. 1, 3–6, 24, 29, 31, 39)*.

1 Corinthians 13:10-12 declares, "but when perfection comes, the imperfect disappears. When I was a child, I talked like a child, I thought like a child, I reasoned like a child. When I became a man, I put childish ways behind me. Now we see but a poor reflection as in a mirror; then we shall see face to face. Now I know in part; then I shall know fully, even as I am fully known."

When shall we see face to face? When shall we know fully, even as we are fully known? This will occur when we pass from this life and enter God's glorious presence in Heaven. *1 John 3:2 tells us, "Dear friends, now we are children of God, and what we will be has not yet been made known. But we know that when he appears, we shall be like him, for we shall see him as he is."* It is when we are glorified in Heaven that we will truly have put childish ways behind us.

15. Question: "What does it mean to grieve/quench the Holy Spirit?"

When the word "quench" is used in Scripture, it is speaking of suppressing fire. When the believers put on the shield of faith, as part of their armor of God *(Ephesians 6:16)*, they are suppressing the power of the fiery darts from Satan. Christ described hell as a place where the fire would not be "quenched" *(Mark 9:44, 46, 48)*. Likewise, the Holy Spirit is a fire dwelling in each believer. He wants to express Himself in our actions and attitudes. When believers do not allow the Spirit to be seen in their actions, when we do what we know is wrong, then we suppress or "quench" the Spirit. We do not allow the Spirit to reveal Himself the way that He wants to.

To understand what it means to "grieve" the Spirit, we must first understand that this is a personality trait. Only a person can be "grieved"; therefore, the Spirit must be a person in order to have this emotion. Once we understand this aspect, we can better understand how He is "grieved," mainly because we, too, are grieved. Ephesians 4:30 tells us that we should not "grieve" the Spirit. Let's stay in the passage to understand what Paul wants to tell us. We can 'grieve' the Spirit by living like the pagans *(4:17-19)*, by yielding to our sin nature *(4:22-24)*, by lying *(4:25)*, by anger *(4:26-27)*, by stealing *(4:28)*, by cursing *(4:29)*, by bitterness *(4:31)*, by being unforgiving *(4:32)*, by sexual immorality *(5:3-5)*. To "grieve" the Spirit is to act out in a sinful manner, whether it is in thought and deed, or in thought only.

Both "quenching" and "grieving" the Spirit are similar in their effects; both hinder a godly lifestyle. Both happen when a believer sins against God and follows his or her own worldly desires. The only correct road to follow is the road that leads the believer closer to God and purity, and further away from the world and sin. Just as we do not like to be grieved, and just as we do not seek to quench what is good, so we should not grieve or quench the Holy Spirit by refusing to listen to His leading.

16. Question: "Is speaking in tongues evidence for having the Holy Spirit?"

There are three occasions in the book of Acts where speaking in tongues accompanied the receiving of the Holy Spirit *(Acts 2:4; 10:44-46; 19:6)*. However, these three occasions are the only places in the Bible where speaking in Tongues is an evidence of receiving the Holy Spirit. Throughout the book of *Acts* thousands of people believe in Jesus and nothing is said about them speaking in tongues *(Acts 2:41; 8:5-25; 16:31-34; 21:20)*. Nowhere in the New Testament is it taught that speaking in tongues is the only evidence a person has received the Holy Spirit. In fact, the New Testament teaches the opposite. We are told that every believer in Christ has the Holy Spirit *(Romans 8:9; 1 Corinthians 12:13; Ephesians 1:13-14)*, but not every believer speaks in tongues *(1 Corinthians 12:29-31)*.

So, why was speaking in tongues the evidence of the Holy Spirit in those three passages in *Acts*? *Acts chapter 2* records the apostles being baptized in the Holy Spirit and empowered by Him to proclaim the Gospel. The Apostles were enabled to speak in other languages (tongues) so they could share the truth with people in their own languages. *Acts 10* records the Apostle Peter being sent to share the Gospel with non-Jewish people. Peter and the other early Christians, being Jews, would have a hard time accepting Gentiles (non-Jewish people) into the church. God enabled the Gentiles to speak in tongues to demonstrate that they had received the same Holy Spirit that the apostles had received *(Acts 10:47; 11:17)*.

Acts 10:44-47 describes this; *"While Peter was still speaking these words, the Holy Spirit came on all who heard the message. The circumcised believers who had come with Peter were astonished that the gift of the Holy Spirit had been poured out even on the Gentiles. For they heard them speaking in tongues and praising God. Then Peter said, 'Can anyone keep these people from being baptized with water? They have received the Holy Spirit just as we have.'"* Peter later points back to this occasion as proof that God was indeed saving the Gentiles *(Acts 15:7-11)*.

Speaking in tongues is not presented anywhere in the Bible as something Christians should expect when they receive Jesus Christ as their Savior and are therefore baptized in the Holy Spirit. In fact, out of all the conversion accounts in the New Testament, only two record speaking in tongues in that context. Tongues was a miraculous gift that had a specific purpose for a specific time. It was not, and never has been, the evidence of the reception of the Holy Spirit.

17. Question: "What is the fruit of the Holy Spirit?"

Galatians 5:22-23 tells us, *"But the fruit of the Spirit is love, joy, peace, patience, kindness, goodness, faithfulness, gentleness and self-control..."* The fruit of the Holy Spirit are the results of the Holy Spirit taking a role in the life of a Christian. The Bible makes it clear that everyone receives the Holy Spirit the moment he or she believes in Jesus Christ *(Romans 8:9; 1 Corinthians 12:13; Ephesians 1:13-14)*. One of the primary purposes of the Holy Spirit coming into a Christian's life is to change that life. It is the Holy Spirit's job to conform us to the image of Christ, making us more like Him.

The fruit of the Holy Spirit are in direct contrast with the acts of the sinful nature in *Galatians 5:19-21, "The acts of the sinful nature are obvious: sexual immorality, impurity and debauchery; idolatry and witchcraft; hatred, discord, jealousy, fits of rage, selfish ambition, dissensions, factions and envy; drunkenness, orgies, and the like. I warn you, as I did before, that those who live like this will not inherit the kingdom of God." Galatians 5:19-21* is what people are like, to varying degrees, when they do not know Christ and therefore are not under the influence of the Holy Spirit. Our sinful flesh produces types of fruit *(Galatians 5:19-21)*, and the Holy Spirit produces types of fruit *(Galatians 5:22-23)*.

The Christian life is a battle of the acts of the sinful nature with the fruit of the Holy Spirit. As fallen human beings, we are still trapped in a body that desires sinful things *(Romans 7:14-25)*. As Christians, we have the Holy Spirit producing His fruit in us and the Holy Spirit's power available to us to conquer the acts of the sinful nature *(2 Corinthians 5:17; Philippians 4:13)*. A Christian will never be completely victorious in always demonstrating the fruits of the Holy Spirit. It is one of the main purposes of the Christian life, though, to progressively allow the Holy Spirit to produce more and more of His fruit in our lives, and to allow the Holy Spirit to conquer the opposing sinful desires. The fruit of the Spirit is what God desires our lives to look like...and with the Holy Spirit's help, it is possible!

18. Question: "Is a believer supposed to be able to feel the Holy Spirit?"

While certain ministries of the Holy Spirit may involve a "feeling," such as conviction of sin, comfort, and empowerment. Scripture does not instruct us to base our relationship with the Holy Spirit on how or what we feel. Every born-again believer has the indwelling Holy Spirit. Jesus told us that when the Comforter has come He will be with us and in us. *"And I will pray the Father, and He shall give you another Comforter, that He may abide with you forever; Even the Spirit of truth; whom the world cannot receive, because it seeth Him not, neither knoweth Him: but ye know Him; for He dwelleth with you, and shall be in you" (John 14:16-17)*. In other words, Jesus is sending one like Himself to be with us and in us.

We know the Holy Spirit is with us because God's Word tells us that it is so. Every born-again believer is indwelt by the Holy Spirit, but not every believer is "controlled" by the Holy Spirit, and there is a distinct difference. When we step out in our flesh, we are not under the control of the Holy Spirit even though we are still indwelt by Him. The Apostle Paul comments on this truth, and he uses an illustration that helps us to understand. *"And be not drunk with wine, wherein is excess; but be filled with the Spirit" (Ephesians 5:18)*. Many people read this verse and interpret it to mean that the Apostle Paul is speaking against wine. However, the context of this passage is the walk and the warfare of the Spirit-filled believer. Therefore, there is something more here than just a warning about drinking too much wine.

When people are drunk with too much wine, they exhibit certain characteristics: they reel, their speech is slurred, and their judgment is impaired. The Apostle Paul sets up a comparison here. Just as there are certain characteristics that allow us to see that someone is controlled by too much wine, there should also be certain characteristics that allow us to see that someone is being controlled by the Holy Spirit. We read in *Galatians 5:22-24* about the "fruit" of the Spirit. This is His fruit, and it is exhibited by the born-again believer who walks under the control of the Spirit.

The verb tense in *Ephesians 5:18* indicates a continual process of being filled by the Holy Spirit. Since it is an exhortation "be being filled," it follows that it is also possible not to be "filled" or controlled by the Spirit. The rest of *Ephesians 5* gives us the characteristics of a Spirit-filled believer. *"Speaking to yourselves in psalms and hymns and spiritual songs, singing and making melody in your heart to the Lord; Giving thanks always for all things unto God and the Father in the name of our Lord Jesus Christ; Submitting yourselves one to another in the fear of God" (Ephesians 5:19-21).*

Therefore, the born-again believer should not be controlled by anything other than the Holy Spirit. We are not filled with the Spirit because we "feel" we are, but because this is the privilege and possession we have in Christ. Being filled or controlled by the Spirit is the result of walking in obedience to the LORD. This is a gift of grace and not an emotional feeling. Emotions can and will deceive us, and we can work ourselves up into an emotional frenzy that is purely from the flesh and not of the Holy Spirit. *"This I say then, Walk in the Spirit, and ye shall not fulfill the lust of the flesh. If we live in the Spirit, let us also walk in the Spirit" (Galatians 5:16, 25).*

Having said that, we cannot discount that there are times when we can be overwhelmed by the presence and the power of the Spirit, and this is often an emotional experience. When that happens, it is a joy like no other. King David *"danced for joy" (2 Samuel 6:14)* when they brought up the Ark of the Covenant to Jerusalem. Experiencing joy by the Spirit is the understanding that as children of God we are being blessed by His grace. So, absolutely, the ministries of the Holy Spirit can involve our feelings and emotions. At the same time, while the Holy Spirit's work in our lives can include a "feeling," we are not to base the assurance of our possession of the Holy Spirit on how we feel.

19. Question: "What is praying in the Spirit?"

Praying in the Spirit is mentioned three times in Scripture. *1 Corinthians 14:15* says, *"So what shall I do? I will pray with my spirit, but I will also pray with my mind; I will sing with my spirit, but I will also sing with my mind." Ephesians 6:18* says, *"And pray in the Spirit on all occasions with all kinds of prayers and requests. With this in mind, be alert and always keep on praying for all the saints." Jude 20* says, *"But you, dear friends, build yourselves up in your most holy faith and pray in the Holy Spirit."* Some Christians understand these Scriptures to be referring to praying in tongues, a view which is not supportable scripturally.

The Greek word translated "pray in" the Spirit can have several different meanings. It can mean "by means of," "with the help of," "in the sphere of," and "in connection to." Praying in the Spirit does not refer to the words we are saying. Rather, it refers to how we are praying. Praying in the Spirit is praying according to the Spirit's leading. It is praying for things that the Spirit leads us to pray for. *Romans 8:26* tells us, *"In the same way, the Spirit helps us in our weakness. We do not know what we ought to pray for, but the Spirit Himself intercedes for us with groans that words cannot express."*

Perhaps the primary reason praying in the Spirit is linked with tongues is *1 Corinthians 14:15*. In the context of discussing the gift of tongues, Paul mentions *"pray with my spirit." 1 Corinthians 14* repeatedly states that when a person speaks in tongues, while he knows what he is saying, since it is spoken in a language he does not know, no one can understand what he is saying...unless someone interprets for him. In *Ephesians 6:18*, Paul instructs us to *"pray in the Spirit on all occasions with all kinds of prayers and requests."* How are we to pray with all kinds of prayers and requests and pray for the saints if no one understands what is being said? Therefore, praying in the Spirit should be understood as praying in the power of the Spirit and according to His will, not as praying in tongues.

20. Question: "Will the Holy Spirit ever leave a believer?"

Simply put, no, the Holy Spirit will never leave a believer. This truth is revealed in many different passages in the New Testament. For example, *Romans 8:9* tells us, *"If anyone does not have the Spirit of Christ, he is not His."* This verse is very clear that if someone does not have the indwelling presence of the Holy Spirit, then he/she is not saved; therefore, if the Holy Spirit were to leave a believer, he/she would have lost his/her relationship with Christ and lost his/her salvation. Yet this is clearly contrary to what the Bible teaches about the "eternal security" of Christians. Another verse that speaks clearly to the permanence of the Holy Spirit's indwelling presence in the life of believers is *John 14:16*. Here Jesus states that the Father will give another Helper and that *"He may be with you forever."*

The fact that the Holy Spirit will never leave a believer is also seen in *Ephesians 1:13-14* where believers are said to be *"sealed"* with the Holy Spirit, *"who is given as a pledge of our inheritance with a view to the redemption of God's own possession, to the praise of His glory."* The picture of being sealed with the Spirit is one of ownership and possession. God has promised eternal life to all who believe in Christ, and as a guarantee that He will keep His promise, He has sent the Holy Spirit to indwell the believer until the day of redemption. Similar to making a down payment on a car or a house, God has provided all believers with a down payment of their future relationship with Him by sending the Holy Spirit to indwell them. The fact that all believers are sealed with the Spirit is also seen in *2 Corinthians 1:22* and *Ephesians 4:30*.

Prior to Christ's death, resurrection, and ascension into Heaven, the Holy Spirit had a "come and go" relationship with people. The Holy Spirit indwelt King Saul, but then departed from him *(1 Samuel 16:14)*. Instead, the Spirit came upon David *(1 Samuel 16:13)*. After his adultery with Bathsheba, David feared that the Holy Spirit would be taken from him *(Psalm 51:11)*. The Holy Spirit filled Bezaleel to enable him to produce the items needed for the tabernacle *(Exodus 31:2-5)*, but this is not described as a permanent relationship. All of this changed after Jesus' ascension into Heaven. Beginning on the day of Pentecost *(Acts 2)*, the Holy Spirit began permanently indwelling believers. The permanent indwelling of the Holy Spirit is the fulfillment of God's promise to always be with us, and never forsake us.

While the Holy Spirit will never leave a believer, it is possible for our sin to *"quench the Holy Spirit" (1 Thessalonians 5:19)* or *"grieve the Holy Spirit" (Ephesians 4:30)*. Sin always has consequences in our relationship with God. While our relationship with God is secure in Christ, unconfessed sin in our lives can hinder our fellowship with God and effectively quench the Holy Spirit's working in our lives. That is why it is so important to confess our sins because God is *"faithful and just to forgive us our sins and to cleanse us from all unrighteousness" (1 John 1:9)*. So, while the Holy Spirit will never leave us, the benefits and joy of His presence can in fact depart from us.

21. Question: "What is the filioque clause/filioque controversy?"

The filioque clause was, and still is, a controversy in the church in relation to the Holy Spirit. The question is, from whom did the Holy Spirit proceed, the Father, or the Father and the Son. The word "filioque" means "and son" in Latin. It is referred to as the filioque "clause" because the phrase "and son" was added to the Nicene Creed, indicating that the Holy Spirit proceeded from the Father "and Son." There was so much contention over this issue that it eventually led to the split between the Roman Catholic and Eastern Orthodox churches in A.D. 1054. The two churches are still not in agreement on the filioque clause.

John 14:26 tells us, *"But the Counselor, the Holy Spirit, whom the Father will send in my name..." John 15:26* tells us, *"When the Counselor comes, whom I will send to you from the Father, the Spirit of truth who goes out from the Father, He will testify about me."* See also *John 14:16* and *Philippians 1:19*. These Scriptures seem to indicate that the Spirit is sent out by both the Father and the Son. The essential matter in the filioque clause is a desire to protect the deity of the Holy Spirit. The Bible clearly teaches that the Holy Spirit is God *(Acts 5:3-4)*. Those who oppose the filioque clause object because they believe the Holy Spirit proceeding from the Father and the Son makes the Holy Spirit "subservient" to the Father and Son. Those who uphold the filioque clause believe that the Holy Spirit proceeding from both the Father and the Son does not impact the Spirit being equally God with the Father and the Son.

The filioque clause controversy is likely an aspect of God's person that we will never be able to fully grasp. God, being an infinite being, is ultimately incomprehensible to us finite human beings. The Holy Spirit is God. He was sent by God as Jesus Christ's "replacement" here on earth. Whether the Holy Spirit was sent by the Father or the Father and the Son likely cannot be decisively answered, nor does it absolutely need to be answered. The filioque clause will perhaps have to remain a controversy.

22. Question: "Is cessationism Biblical?"

Cessationism is the view that the "miracle gifts" of tongues and healing have ceased, that the end of the apostolic age brought about a cessation of the miracles associated with that age. Most cessationists believe that, while God can and still does perform miracles today, the Holy Spirit no longer uses individuals to perform miraculous signs.

The biblical record shows that miracles occurred during particular periods for the specific purpose of authenticating a new message from God. Moses was enabled to perform miracles to authenticate his ministry before Pharaoh *(Exodus 4:1-8)*; Elijah was given miracles to authenticate his ministry before Ahab *(1 Kings 17:1; 18:24)*; the apostles were given miracles to authenticate their ministry before Israel *(Acts 4:10, 16)*.

Jesus' ministry was also marked by miracles, which the Apostle John calls *"signs" (John 2:11)*. John's point is that the miracles were proofs of the authenticity of Jesus' message.

After Jesus' resurrection, as the Church was being established and the New Testament was being written, the apostles demonstrated "signs" such as tongues and the power to heal. *"Tongues are for a sign, not to them that believe, but to them that believe not" (1 Corinthians 14:22)* This verse that plainly says the gift was never intended to edify the church).

The Apostle Paul predicted that the gift of tongues would cease *(1 Corinthians 13:8)*. Here are 6 proofs that it has already ceased:

1. The apostles, through whom tongues came, were unique in the history of the church. Once their ministry was accomplished, the need for authenticating signs ceased to exist.
2. The miracle (or sign) gifts are only mentioned in the earliest Epistles, such as *1 Corinthians*. Later books, such as *Ephesians* and *Romans*, contain detailed passages on the gifts of the Spirit, but the miracle gifts are not mentioned. Although Romans does mention the gift of prophecy, the Greek word translated prophecy mean "speaking forth" and does not necessarily include prediction of the future.
3. The gift of tongues was a sign to unbelieving Israel that God's salvation was now available to other nations. See *1 Corinthians 14:21-22* and *Isaiah 28:11-12*.
4. Tongues was an inferior gift to prophecy (preaching). Preaching the Word of God edifies believers, whereas tongues does not. Believers are told to seek prophesying over speaking in tongues *(1 Corinthians 14:1-3)*.
5. History indicates that tongues did cease. Tongues are not mentioned at all by the Post-Apostolic Fathers. Other writers such as Justin Martyr, Origen, Chrysostom, and Augustine considered tongues something that happened only in the earliest days of the Church.
6. Current observation confirms that the miracle of tongues has ceased. If the gift were still available today, there would be no need for missionaries to attend language school. Missionaries would be able to travel to any country and speak any language fluently, just as the apostles were able to speak in *Acts 2*. As for the miracle gift of healing, we see in Scripture that healing was associated with the ministry of Jesus and the apostles *(Luke 9:1-2)*. And we see that as the era of the apostles drew to a close, healing, like tongues, became less frequent. The Apostle Paul, who raised Eutychus from the dead *(Acts 20:9-12)*, did not heal Epaphroditus *(Philippians 2:25-27)*, Trophimus *(2 Timothy 4:20)*, Timothy *(1 Timothy 5:23)*, or even himself *(2 Corinthians 12:7-9)*. The reasons for Paul's "failures to heal" are:
    a. the gift was never intended to make every Christian well, but to authenticate apostleship; and

b. the authority of the apostles had been sufficiently proved, making further miracles unnecessary.

The reasons stated above are evidence that the sign gifts have ceased. According to *1 Corinthians 13:13-14:1*, we would do well to *"pursue love,"* the greatest gift of all. If we are to desire gifts, we should desire to speak forth the Word of God, that all may be edified.

23. Question: "What is the difference between the Holy Spirit and Holy Ghost?"

It is only the King James Version of the Bible which uses the term "Holy Ghost." It occurs 90 times in the KJV. The term "Holy Spirit" occurs 7 times in the KJV. There is no clear reason as to why the KJV translators used Ghost in most places and then Spirit in a few. The exact same Greek and Hebrew words are translated "ghost" and "spirit" in the KJV in different occurrences of the words. By "ghost," the KJV translators did not intend to communicate the idea of "the spirit of a deceased person." In 1611, when the KJV was originally translated, the word "ghost" primarily referred to "an immaterial being."

With recent Scripture translations, "Spirit" has replaced "Ghost" in most instances. Some of this came about because words don't always hold their meanings. In the days of Shakespeare or King James, ghost meant the living essence of a person. Looking back, we see that the words "breath" or "soul" were often used as synonyms of "ghost." During these times, spirit normally meant the essence of a departed person or a demonic or paranormal apparition. As language evolved, people started saying "ghost" when speaking of the vision of a dead person while "spirit" became the standard term for life or living essence, often also for "soul." With slight exceptions, "ghost" and "spirit" changed places over some 300 years.

The real issue is that both "Holy Ghost" and "Holy Spirit" refer to the Third Person of the Trinity, coequal and consubstantial with the Father and the Son *(Matthew 28:19; Acts 5:3,4; 28:25,26; 1 Corinthians 12:4 -6)*. He is the gift of the Father to His people on earth to initiate and complete the building of the body of Christ *(1 Corinthians 12:13)*. He is also the agency by which the world is convicted of sin, the Lord Jesus is glorified, and believers are transformed into His image *(John 16:7-9; Acts 1:5, 2:4; Romans 8:29; 2 Corinthians 3:18; Ephesians 2:22)*. Whichever term we use, we remember that this Holy Ghost is God's active breath, blowing where He wishes, creating faith through water and Word.

24. Question: "What does it mean that the Holy Spirit is our Paraclete?"

The time of the arrest and crucifixion of the Lord Jesus Christ was drawing near. As Jesus met with His disciples in the "upper room," He expounded to them many things. In *John 13:33*, He stated: *"My children, I will be with you only a little longer...where I am going you cannot come."* The announcement of the coming separation led to the indication of its purpose. The season of bereavement was to be a season of spiritual growth. To this end Christ gave a commandment designed to lead His disciples to appropriate the lessons of His life, and in so doing, to realize their true character, to follow and to find Him as indicated in *verses 34 and 35*.

In light of their weak faith at this point, Jesus told them in *John 14:1, "Do not let your heart be troubled. Trust in God; trust also in Me..."* Jesus had just explained to them that one of them was a traitor; He had warned Peter that he would deny His Lord three times; and, perhaps the heaviest blow of all was that Jesus was going to leave them *(John 13:33)*. Now He says, *"...let not your heart be troubled" (John 14:1)*. In *John 14:16- 17*, Jesus gives them a statement of great encouragement: *"And I will ask the Father (pray), and He will give you another Counselor to be with you forever...the Spirit of Truth" (NIV)*.

The Greek word translated "Comforter or Counselor" is "Parakletos" as found in *John 14:16, 26; 15:26*; and *16:7*. Once, it is translated "advocate" *(1 John 2:1)*. The New International Version (NIV) has translated the word as Counselor. The form of the word is unquestionably passive. It can properly mean only "one called to the side of another," and that with the secondary notion of counseling or supporting or aiding him. The contexts in which the word "paraclete" occurs in the New Testament lead to the same conclusions as the form and the independent usage of the word. In *1 John 2:1*, the sense "Advocate" alone suits the argument, though the Greek fathers explain the term as applied to the Lord in the same way as in the Gospel. In the Gospel again, the sense of Advocate, counsel, one who pleads, convinces, convicts, who strengthens on the one hand and defends on the other, is alone adequate. Christ as the Advocate pleads the believer's cause with the Father against the accuser Satan (*1 John 2:1*; compare *Romans 8:26, Revelation 12:10* and also *Zechariah 3:1*). The Holy Spirit (Parakletos) as the Advocate pleads the believer's cause against the world *(John 16:8ff)* and also Christ's cause with the believer *(John 14:26; 15:26; 16:14)*.

By saying what He did to His disciples, Jesus was comforting their troubled hearts. In *14:16* He states: *"I will pray to the Father and He will send you another Comforter"* – paraklete, another is 'heteros", one of the same kind, which is the Holy Spirit. First of all, this paraclete is God the Holy Spirit, the third person of the Trinity. He is a true personality and a personal being. He indwells every believer. He has been called in some translations "Encourager." As the "Spirit of Truth," the Holy Spirit illumines the Word of God so believers may understand it. He leads us in that truth of God's Word. He uses the Word of truth to guide us into the will and the work of God.

The Holy Spirit abides in every believer. He is a gift from the Father in answer to the prayer of the Son *(verse 16)*. During His earthly ministry, Jesus had guided, guarded, and taught His disciples, but now He was going to leave them. The Spirit of God would come to them and dwell in them, taking the place of their Master's literal presence. Jesus called the Spirit "another Comforter, another of the same kind". The Spirit of God is not different from the Son of God for both are God (One in essence). The Spirit of God had dwelt with the disciples in the Person of Jesus Christ. Now He would dwell in them.

During the Old Testament Age, the Spirit of God would come on people and then leave them. God's Spirit departed from King Saul *(1 Samuel 16:14; 18:12)*; and David, when confessing his sin, asked that the Spirit not be taken from him *(Psalm 51:11)*. When the Spirit was given at Pentecost, He was given to God's people to remain with them forever. Even though we may grieve the Holy Spirit, He will not leave us.

Jesus said in *Matthew 28:20 "...And surely I am with always, to the very end of the age."* How is He with us when we are taught that He is in Heaven, seated at the right hand of the Father? He is with us by His Spirit (the other of the same kind, the Parakletos, the Comforter, the Advocate), who indwells us and never will leave us if we are true believers in Jesus Christ.

To have the Holy Spirit as our "Paraclete" is to have God Himself indwelling us as believers. He teaches us the Word and guides us into the truth of that Word. He also reminds us of what He has taught us so that we can depend on God's Word in the difficult times of life. The Spirit uses the Word to give us His peace *(John 14:27)*, His love *(John 15:9, 10)*, and His joy *(John 15:11)*. These are profound truths that comfort our hearts and minds in a troubled world. The power of this indwelling "paraclete" gives us the ability to *"live by the Spirit so that we will not gratify the desires of the sinful flesh"* and *"Since we live by the Spirit, let us keep in step with the Spirit" (Galatians 5:16, 25)*. We, then, can have the *"fruit of the Spirit"* produced in our own lives *(Galatians 5:22, 23)* to the glory of God the Father. What a blessing to have the Holy Spirit in our lives as our "paraclete," our Comforter, our Encourager, our Counselor, and our Advocate. Thank you, Father, for your wonderful gift!

25. Question: "What is the Latter Rain Movement?"

The Latter Rain Movement is an influence within Pentecostalism which teaches that the Lord is pouring out His Spirit again, as He did at Pentecost, and using believers to prepare the world for His Second Coming. The Latter Rain Movement is anti-dispensational and amillennial, and many leaders of the movement embrace aberrant teachings.

The term "latter rain" was first used early in the history of Pentecostalism, when David Wesley Myland wrote a book called Latter Rain Songs in 1907. Three years later, Myland wrote The Latter Rain Covenant, a defense of Pentecostalism in general.

The name comes from *Joel 2:23, "Be glad then, ye children of Zion, and rejoice in the LORD your God: for He hath given you the former rain moderately, and He will cause to come down for you the rain, the former rain, and the latter rain in the first month."* Pentecostals interpreted the "rain" in this verse as an outpouring of the Holy Spirit. The "latter rain" (the end-times outpouring) would be greater than the "former rain."

In 1948, a "revival" broke out in Saskatchewan, Canada, and the teachings of the Latter Rain Movement were clarified. Those involved in the revival were convinced that they were on the verge of a new era, one in which the Holy Spirit would demonstrate His power in a greater way than the world had ever seen. Not even the age of the apostles, they said, had witnessed such a movement of the Holy Spirit.

Latter Rain teaching is characterized by a highly typological hermeneutic. That is, the Bible is interpreted in a symbolic, extremely stylized manner. An emphasis is placed on extra-biblical revelation, such as personal prophecies and directives straight from God. Latter Rain doctrine includes the following beliefs:

- the gifts of the Spirit, including tongues, are received through the laying on of hands
- Christians can be demonized and require deliverance
- God has restored all the offices of ministry to the Church, including apostle and prophet
- divine healing can be administered through the laying on of hands
- praise and worship will usher God into our presence
- women have a full and equal ministry role in the Church
- denominational lines will be destroyed, and the Church will unify in the last days
- the "latter rain" will bring God's work to completion; the Church will be victorious over the world and usher in Christ's kingdom

Many "apostles" in the Latter Rain Movement also teach the doctrine of "the manifest sons of God." This is a heretical doctrine which says that the Church will give rise to a special group of "overcomers" who will receive spiritual bodies, becoming immortal.

It is important to note that the Assemblies of God deemed the Latter

Rain Movement to contain heresy from the very beginning. On April 20, 1949, the Assemblies of God officially denounced Latter Rain teaching, nearly splitting the denomination in the process. Other established Pentecostal groups have passed similar resolutions.

Today, the term "latter rain" is rarely used, but the theology of Latter Rain continues to exert an influence. Most branches of the Charismatic Movement adhere to Latter Rain teaching. Modern movements such as the Brownsville/Pensacola Revival, the Toronto Blessing, and the "holy laughter" phenomenon are a direct result of Latter Rain theology.

26. Question: "What is praying in tongues? Is praying in tongues a prayer language between a believer and God?"

As a background, please read our article on the gift of speaking in tongues. There are four primary Scripture passages that are used as evidence for praying in tongues: *Romans 8:26; 1 Corinthians 14:4-17; Ephesians 6:18;* and *Jude verse 20. Ephesians 6:18* and *Jude verse 20* mention "praying in the Spirit." Tongues as a prayer language is not a likely interpretation of "praying in the Spirit." Please read **What is praying in the Spirit?** for more information.

Romans 8:26 teaches us, *"Likewise the Spirit also helps in our weaknesses. For we do not know what we should pray for as we ought, but the Spirit Himself makes intercession for us with groanings which cannot be uttered."* Two key points make it highly unlikely that *Romans 8:26* is referring to tongues as a prayer language.

   a.   *Romans 8:26* states that it is the Spirit who is "groaning," not believers.
   b.   *Romans 8:26* states that the groanings of the Spirit "cannot be uttered." The very essence of speaking in tongues is uttering words.

That leaves us with *1 Corinthians 14:4-17* and *verse 14* especially, *"For if I pray in a tongue, my spirit prays, but my mind is unfruitful."* *1 Corinthians 14:14* distinctly mentions "praying in tongues." What does this mean? First, studying the context is immensely valuable. *1 Corinthians 14* is primarily a compare/contrast of the gift of speaking in tongues and the gift of prophecy. *Verses 2-5* make it clear that Paul views prophecy as a superior gift to tongues. At the same time, Paul exclaims the value of tongues and declares that he is glad that he speaks in tongues more than anyone *(verse 18)*.

Acts 2 describes the first occurrence of the gift of tongues. On the day of Pentecost, the apostles spoke in tongues. *Acts 2* makes it clear that the apostles were speaking in human languages *(Acts 2:6-8)*. The word translated "tongues" in both *Acts 2* and *1 Corinthians 14* is "glossa" which means "language." Speaking in tongues was the ability to speak in a language one did not know, in order to communicate the Gospel to someone who did speak that language. In the multi-cultural, multi-language area of Corinth, it seems that the gift of tongues was especially valuable and prominent. As a result of the gift of tongues, the Corinthian believers were able to better communicate the Gospel and God's Word to those who spoke other languages. However, Paul made it abundantly clear that even in this usage of tongues, it was necessary to be interpreted or "translated" *(1 Corinthians 14:13,27)*. A Corinthian believer would speak in tongues, ministering God's truth to someone who spoke that language, and then that believer, or another believer in the church, was to interpret what was spoken, so the entire assembly could understand what was said.

What, then, is "praying in tongues" and how is it different from speaking in tongues? *1 Corinthians 14:13-17* indicates that praying in tongues is also to be interpreted. As a result, it seems that praying in tongues was offering a prayer to God. This prayer would minister to someone who spoke that language, but would also need to be interpreted so that the entire body could be edified.

This interpretation does not agree with those who view praying in tongues as a personal prayer language. This alternate understanding can be summarized as praying in tongues is a personal prayer language between a believer and God *(1 Corinthians 13:1)* that a believer uses to edify himself *(1 Corinthians 14:4)*. This interpretation is unbiblical for the following reasons:

1. How could praying in tongues be a private prayer language if it is to be interpreted *(1 Corinthians 14:13-17)*?
2. How could praying in tongues be for self-edification when

Scripture says that the spiritual gifts are for the edification of the church, not the self *(1 Corinthians 12:7)*.

3. How can praying in tongues be a private prayer language if tongues is a "sign to unbelievers" *(1 Corinthians 14:22)*?

4. The Bible makes it clear that not everyone possesses the gift of tongues *(1 Corinthians 12:11,28-30)*. How could tongues be a gift for self-edification if not every believer can possess it? Do we not all need to be edified?

There is an additional understanding of praying in tongues that needs to be addressed. Some understand praying in tongues to be a "secret code language" that prevents Satan and his demons from understanding our prayers, and thereby gaining an advantage over us. This interpretation is unbiblical for the following reasons:

1. The New Testament consistently describes tongues as a human language. It is unlikely that Satan and his demons are unable to understand human languages.

2. The Bible records countless believers praying in their own language, out loud, with no concern of Satan intercepting the prayer. Even if Satan and/or his demons heard and understood the prayers we pray, they have absolutely no power to prevent God from answering the prayer according to His will. We know that God hears our prayers, and that fact makes it irrelevant whether Satan and his demons hear and understand our prayers.

With all of that said, what of the many Christians who have experienced praying in tongues and find it to be very edifying for themselves?

- First, we must base our faith and practice on Scripture, not experience. We must view our experiences in light of Scripture, not interpret Scripture in light of our experiences.

- Second, many of the cults and world religions also report occurrences of speaking and/or praying in tongues. Obviously the Holy Spirit is not gifting these unbelieving individuals. So it seems that the demons are able to counterfeit the gift of speaking in tongues. This should cause us to even more carefully compare our experiences with Scripture.

- Third, many studies have shown how speaking / praying in

tongues can be a learned behavior. Through hearing and observing others speak in tongues, a person can learn the procedure, even subconsciously. This is the most likely explanation for the vast majority of instances of speaking / praying in tongues among Christians.

- Fourth, the feeling of "self-edification" is natural. The human body produces adrenaline and endorphins when it experiences something new, exciting, emotionally-induced, and/or disconnected from rational thought.

Praying in tongues is most definitely an issue on which Christians can respectfully and lovingly agree to disagree. Praying in tongues is not what determines salvation. Praying in tongues is not what separates a mature Christian from an immature Christian. Whether or not praying in tongues is a prayer language is not a fundamental of the Christian faith. So while we believe the Biblical interpretation of praying in tongues leads away from the idea of a private prayer language for personal edification, we also recognize that many who practice such are our brothers and sisters in Christ, and are worthy of our love and respect.

27. Question: "Is the Holy Spirit a "He," "She," or "It," male, female, or neuter?"

A common mistake made with regard to the Holy Spirit is referring to the Spirit as "it," which the Bible never does. This is because the Holy Spirit is a person. He has the attributes of personhood, performs the actions of persons, and has personal relationships. He has insight *(1 Corinthians 2:10-11)*. He knows things, which requires an intellect *(Romans 8:27)*. He has a will *(1 Corinthians 12:11)*. He convicts of sin *(John 16:8)*. He performs miracles *(Acts 8:39)*. He guides *(John 16:13)*. He intercedes between persons *(Romans 8:26)*. He is to be obeyed *(Acts 10:19-20)*. He can be lied to *(Acts 5:3)*, resisted *(Acts 7:51)*, grieved *(Ephesians 4:30)*, blasphemed *(Matthew 12:31)*, even insulted *(Hebrews 10:29)*. He relates to the apostles *(Acts 15:28)* and to each member of the Trinity *(John 16:14; Matthew 28:19; 2 Corinthians 13:14)*. The personhood of the Holy Spirit is presented without question in the Bible, but what about gender?

Linguistically it is abundantly clear that masculine theistic terminology dominates the Scriptures. Throughout both testaments, references to God use masculine pronouns. Specific names for God (e.g., Yahweh, Elohim, Adonai, Kurios, Theos, etc.) are all masculine gender. God is never given a feminine name, or referred to using feminine pronouns. It should be noted, however, that masculine pronouns throughout history have been used for the collective sense of humanity, referring to both male and female. The Holy Spirit is referred to in the masculine throughout the New Testament although the word for "spirit" by itself (pneuma) is actually gender neutral. The Hebrew word for "spirit" (ruach) is feminine in *Genesis 1:2*. But the gender of a word in Greek or Hebrew has nothing to do with gender identity.

Theologically speaking, since the Holy Spirit is God, we can make some statements about Him from general statements about God. God is spirit as opposed to physical or material. God is invisible and spirit, non-body *(John 4:24; Luke 24:39; Romans 1:20; Colossians 1:15; 1 Timothy 1:17)*. This is why no material thing was ever to be used to represent God *(Exodus 20:4)*. If gender is an attribute of the body, it seems that a spirit does not have gender. God, in His essence, has no gender.

Gender identifications of God in the Bible are not unanimous. Many people think that the Bible presents God in exclusively male terms but this is not the case. God is said to give birth in the book of *Job* and portrays Himself as a mother in *Isaiah*. Jesus described the Father as being like a woman in search of a lost coin in *Luke 15* (and Himself as a "mother hen" in *Matthew 23:37*). In *Genesis 1:26-27* God said, *"Let us make humankind in our image, after our likeness,"* and then *"God created humankind in his own image, in the image of God he created them, male and female he created them."* Thus, the image of God was male and female - not simply one or the other. This is further confirmed in *Genesis 5:2* which can be literally translated as *"He created them male and female; when they were created, he blessed them and named them Adam."* The Hebrew term "adam" means "man", the context showing whether it means "man" (as opposed to woman) or "mankind" (in the collective sense). Therefore, to whatever degree humanity is made in the image of God, gender is not an issue.

Masculine imagery and revelation is not without significance, however. A second time that God was specifically said to be revealed via a physical image was when Jesus was asked to show the Father to the disciples in *John 14*. He responds in *verse 8* by saying, *"The person who has seen me has seen the Father!"* Paul makes it clear that Jesus was the exact image of God in *Colossians 1:15* calling Jesus *"the image of the invisible God."* This verse is couched in a section that demonstrates Christ's superiority over all creation. Most ancient religions believed in a pantheon, both gods and goddesses, that were worthy of worship. But one of Judeo-Christianity's distinctive points is its belief in a supreme Creator. Masculine language better relates this relationship of creator to creation. As a man comes into a woman from without to make her pregnant, so God creates the universe from without rather than birthing it from within...As a woman cannot impregnate herself, so the universe cannot create itself. Paul echoes this idea in *1 Timothy 2:12-14* when he refers to the creation order as a template for church order.

In the end, whatever our theological explanation, the fact is that God used exclusively masculine terms to refer to Himself, and almost exclusively masculine terminology even in metaphor. Through the Bible He taught us how to speak of Him and it was in masculine relational terms. So, while the Holy Spirit is neither male nor female in His essence, He is properly referred to in the masculine by virtue of His relation to creation and biblical revelation. There is absolutely no biblical basis for viewing the Holy Spirit as the "female" member of the Trinity.